PORTRAIT SERIES

The Peak Line

A Pictorial Journey compiled by C.W. Judge and J.R. Morten

THE OAKWOOD PRESS

© 1994 Oakwood Press,
C.W. Judge & J.R. Morten
Minor updates and reprint 2021

ISBN 978-0-85361-755-6

Printed by Blissetts, Unit E1-E8
Shield Drive, West Cross Ind Pk,
Brentford, TW8 9EX

The photographs in this book are from the fine collection of negatives by E.R. Morten, Buxton. Tickets are courtesy of John Strange. Thanks to Paul Webster of Community Rail Network for the 2019 photographs of Matlock station. Community Rail Network supports local groups and partnerships to connect their community with their railway. They provide a link with their members to government and industry. They also aim to raise awareness about community rail, its importance, and promote engagement with and travel by community rail.

Title page
Watched by the photographer's son, a clean class '4F' 0-6-0 LMS No. 4050 trundles northwards through Cromford station hauling a very long freight on a hot summer's day in August 1934. Note the Midland Railway's economic use of the signal post with the bi-directional distant signals.

No part of this book may be reproduced or transmitted in any form or by any means, electronic or mechanical, including photocopying, recording or by any information storage and retrieval system, without permission from the publisher in writing. All rights reserved.

The beautiful curves of the Monsal Dale viaduct with the line snaking left to right. hugging the valley sides as it crosses the River Wye and passes through Upper Dale and on towards Cressbrook, typifies the scenery that the passengers encountered as they travelled the Peak Line.

Bibliography

The Railway from Buxton to Bakewell, Matlock and Ambergate by J.M. Bentley, published by Foxline Publishing.
Cromford and High Peak Railway by A. Rimmer, published by the Oakwood Press.
A Pictorial Record of Midland Railway Architecture by V.R. Anderson and G.K. Fox, published by Oxford Publishing Co.
Through Limestone Hills by Bill Hudson, published by Oxford Publishing Co.
The Peak Line by J.M. Stephenson, published by the Oakwood Press.
The use of the *Railway Magazine, Locomotive Magazine* and *Railway World*. All maps unless otherwise captioned are based on the 1922, 25 inch Ordnance Survey maps and are reproduced courtesy, The Ordnance Survey, Southampton, Great Britain.

The Oakwood Press, 54-58 Mill Square, Catrine, KA5 6RD; 01290 551122; www.stenlake.co.uk

Introduction

Two of the many tunnels experienced whilst traversing the Peak Line on its climb from Ambergate to Peak Forest and then on to Chinley. Chee Tor tunnels No. 1 and No. 2, near to Miller's Dale, are seen here from the cab of a diesel multiple unit (dmu) in the 1960s.

'Miller's Dale, change for Buxton' was last heard at the station in 1967, when passenger services all over the country were being brutally reduced (by the Beeching axe); goods facilities had been terminated a year earlier. Part of the picturesque Peak Line still enjoys a passenger service today, namely from Ambergate to Matlock whilst preservationists (Peak Rail PLC) have constructed a new station (Matlock Riverside), relaid a section of track northwards to Darley Dale and operate at weekends and on other days during the summer months, with a long term vision of relaying all the track to Buxton! Some project!

However the remaining sections of the Peak Line, in most cases, can be enjoyed on foot or bicycle, as parts of the trackbed are now used as well kept footpaths. These allow all to enjoy the quietness and to see the wild life, flora and exhilarating scenery which forms the character of the old line as it threads its way through rugged limestone dales of the Peak District.

To climb down to the entrance of Headstone tunnel, amble over the beautiful Monsal viaduct, sit on the platform edge of the lonely Monsal Dale station, wander through Great Longstone station, stand at the foot of the Cromford Incline, walk alongside the Cromford Canal towpath adjacent to the line; all are truly wonderful experiences not to be missed and certainly stimulate inwardly, vivid memories of the steam days past.

This book transports the reader on an imaginary journey from Buxton to Ambergate (with an interlude to Chinley) using photographs dated between 1930 to 1960 from the late E.R. Morten's negatives. Although several of the views have appeared in other works, they are necessary to complete the journey and allow the reader, hopefully, to re-kindle the truly evocative and exciting railway scenes of the past, associated with the Peak Line.

Colin Judge 1994

The Peak Line
CHINLEY
CHAPEL-EN-LE-FRITH
Dove Holes Tunnel
N
PEAK FOREST
Great Rocks Tunnel
Chee Tor Tunnels
BUXTON
MILLER'S DALE
Litton Tunnel
Cressbrook Tunnel
Ashwood Dale Tunnel
BLACKWELL MILL
MONSAL DALE
GREAT LONGSTONE
HASSOP
Chatsworth
Headstone Tunnel
BAKEWELL
Haddon Tunnel
ROWSLEY
DARLEY DALE
Midland Railway
MATLOCK
MATLOCK BATH
High Tor Tunnels
CROMFORD
Willersley Tunnel
Lea Wood Tunnel
WHATSTANDWELL
Whatstandwell Tunnel
AMBERGATE

Tunnel
Ambergate S. Jc
AMBERGATE
Ambergate W. Jc
WHATSTANDWELL
Tunnel
High Peak Jc
Lea Wood Tunnel
CROMFORD
Cromford Tunnel
MATLOCK BATH
High Tor Tunnels
MATLOCK
DARLEY DALE
ROWSLEY
Haddon Tunnel
Haddon Box
BAKEWELL
HASSOP
LONGSTONE
Headstone Tunnel
MONSAL DALE
Cressbrook Tunnel
Litton Tunnel
MILLERS DALE
Chee Tor Tunnels
Millers Dale Jc
Peak Forest Jc
Great Rocks Tunnel
PEAK FOREST
Dove Holes Tunl
L.N.W. Tunnel
CHAPEL-EN-LE-FRITH
Chinley S. Jc
Chinley N. Jc
140
150
160
164

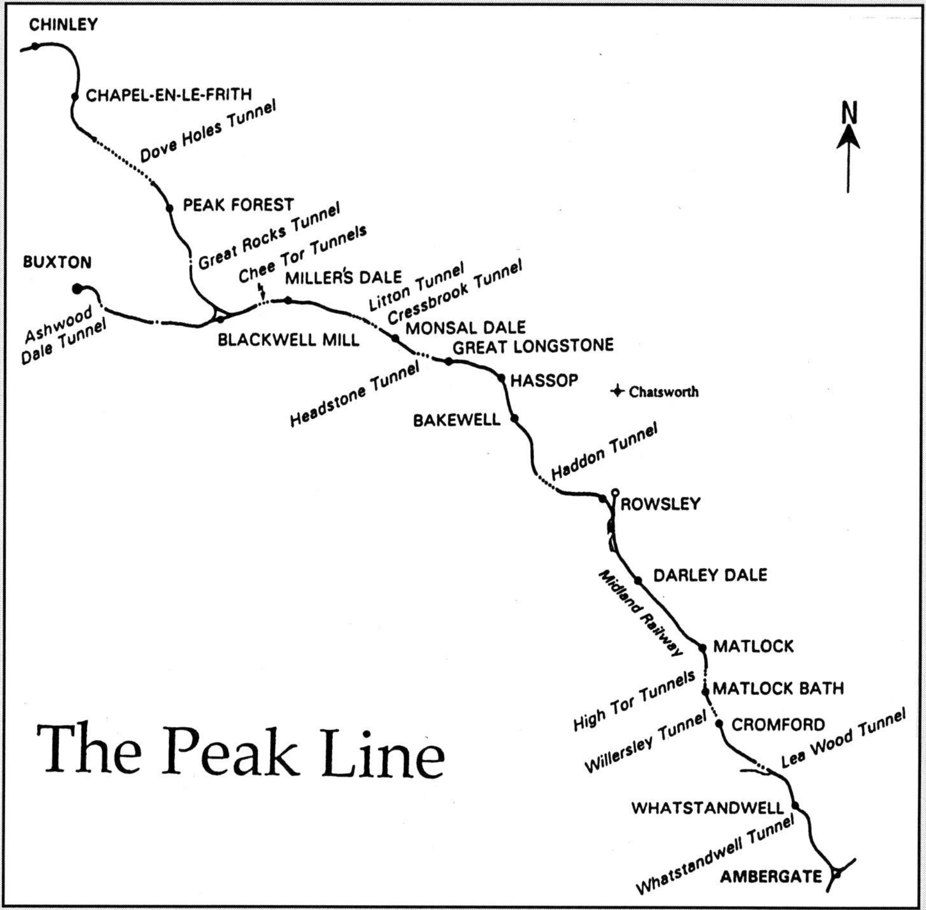

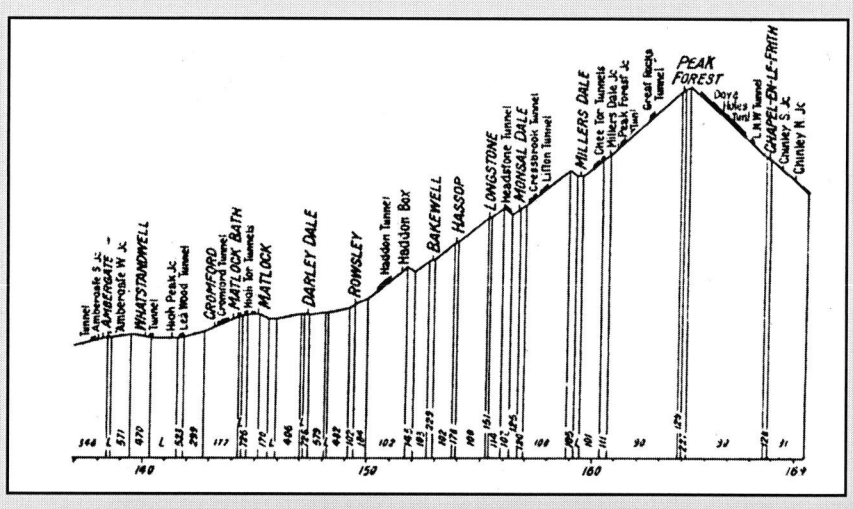

A fine view of Buxton Midland station in September 1950. The area to the left was the site of the old locomotive shed up to 1935. The local two-coach service to Miller's Dale stands in the bay platform, whilst behind can be glimpsed the roof of the LNWR terminus station. The skyline depicts the grandeur of Buxton, with the dome of the Devonshire hospital and the Palace Hotel dominating the scene.

The Midland Railway and London and North Western Railway station façades were once linked by a stone wall with a central gateway, but these were removed in 1927. The nearer end wall of the LNWR station, with its fanlight windows still stands, but the MR station has gone. (*See the next page for picture and a map of the 1920s track layout.*)

This view shows the stone wall between the two stations and the central wooden gate.

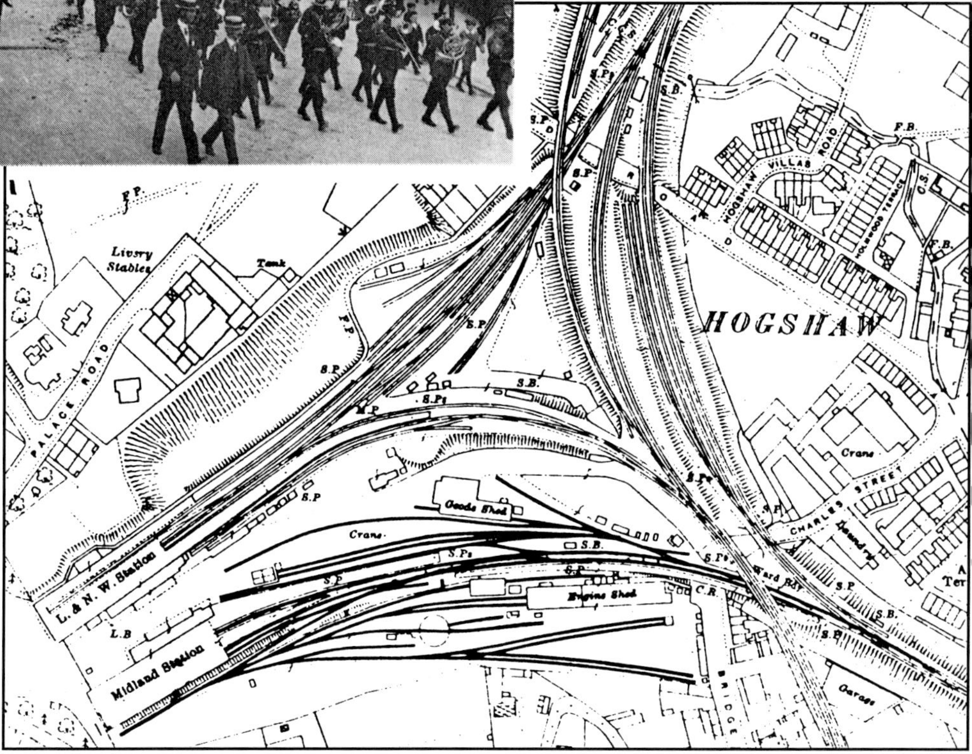

Looking into Buxton Midland station on the 5th October, 1957. The local train to Miller's Dale awaits departure from the bay platform, on the last day of the steam hauled service, whilst a further working stands at platform 5. The wooden structure to the left was a later addition to the 1863 station.

Pulling away from Buxton's platform 4 in October 1957, is class '3F' 0-6-0 No. 43329 with the 9.30 am 'through coach' to London St Pancras. The coach will be attached to the 9.00 am Manchester Central to London express at Miller's Dale. There was a similar return service in the evening. This through coach facility dated back to MR days, and at periods during LMS times there were up to three through coaches per day in each direction.

Class '2P' 4-4-0 No. 447 draws into Buxton Midland station on 11th June, 1932 with the 6.15 pm arrival from Chinley. The station signal box is on the left. The gantry of signals above the box controlled the approach of trains off the LNWR Ashbourne line. The locomotive shed (*right*) had become cramped for space, and in 1935, a single Buxton depot was developed on the site of the ex-LNWR shed.

The introduction of 2-coach 'motor-trains' or push-pull sets, did away with the need for the engine to run round its train. At the height of the service, up to 17 trains per day each way ran between Buxton and Miller's Dale to connect with main line trains.

A Johnson 4-4-0T, No. 1247 (fitted for auto-working), seen here in March 1934 arriving on the local service from Miller's Dale. The train make-up includes a dining car. Note the Barrow-Barnsley Main Colliery private owner wagons standing in the siding. The line abounded with private owner wagons from the many quarries and collieries in the area.

The Buxton to Ashbourne LNWR line crosses the Midland line on Viaduct 158. Through the span of the bridge can be seen Buxton East signal box, whilst this side of the overbridge the Midland line crossed Bridge Street. At Buxton East Junction an alternative line curved off as a spur known as 'the branch' which climbed to join the LNWR.

A two-coach motor train arriving at Buxton from Miller's Dale on 25th July, 1955, with the single through coach from St Pancras attached behind the locomotive, is seen here passing Buxton East signal box. The photographer spent some of his boyhood days in one of the houses to the right, and this nearness to the railway was just one of the formative influences on his love of railways.

Passing Buxton East signal box on 8th August, 1937, the 6.15pm arrival from Chinley consists of just two coaches and is hauled by Fowler 2-6-4T No. 2369. The stop block by the signal box was the scene of a number of incidents over the years, as locomotives travelling down the steeply graded curve on the left, lost control.

A three car dmu is seen here about to enter the Buxton end of Ashwood Dale tunnel (built 1862). This tunnel only 100 yds in length and constructed on a curve, is situated just on the outskirts of Buxton. The headboard reads 'Grimsby Town'.

Johnson Midland class '2P' 4-4-0 No. 447 hurries out of the eastern end of Ashwood Dale tunnel with the 1.28 pm Buxton to Manchester Victoria train in July 1932. The cabin on the left contained a ground frame controlling the Gas works siding in the foreground (*see also map below*).

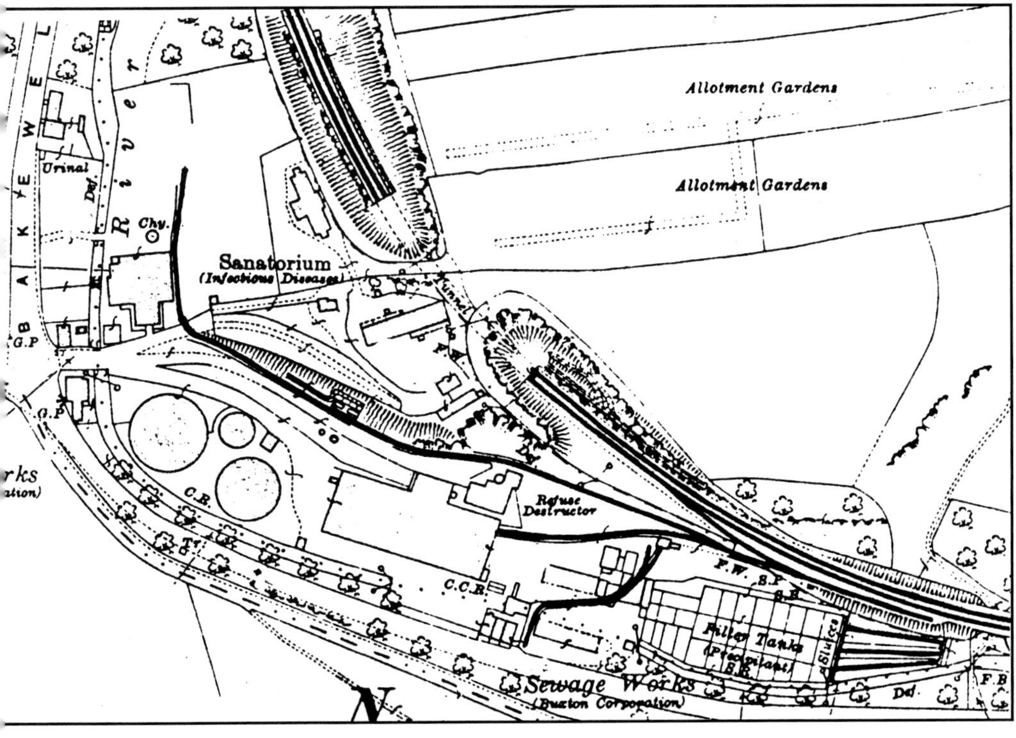

The 5.22 pm from Manchester Central was a long established service to Buxton. The train called at Cheadle Heath, Chinley, Chapel-en-le-Frith and Peak Forest before reaching Buxton. 'Jubilee' class 4-6-0 No. 45650 *Blake* brings the train up the scenic Ashwood Dale on 22nd April, 1951, with about a mile to go to its destination.

Viewed from above Lover's Leap, which was listed as a notable feature of Buxton in early guide books, we see the A6 road and the River Wye 'canalised' here to prevent the erosion of the railway. The train travelling towards Buxton is the push-pull service which has also collected the 'through coach' from London to Buxton, at Miller's Dale.

The local Buxton to Miller's Dale push-pull train with 0-4-4T No. 58084 approaching Ashwood Dale signal box on 22nd May, 1951. Trackwork in connection with quarries sited here, can be seen.

Class '4F' 0-6-0 No. 44231 heading a special from Coalville to Buxton on 14th April, 1952. The train is approaching Ashwood Dale signal box which controlled access to quarries here. On the north side of the line can be seen plant of the Derbyshire Stone Co. Quarry (previously Buxton Lime Firms/ Ashwood Dale Lime and Stone Co.).

Fowler 2-6-4T No. 42368 passes Ashwood Dale signal box on 22nd May, 1951 with the 6.18 pm into Buxton from New Mills. This service waited at Chinley for a connection with a train from Sheffield. The stretch of line here is now reduced to a single line which operates between Buxton and Great Rocks.

The western end of Pie Tor tunnel (191 yards) with 'Jubilee' class 4-6-0 No. 45614 *Leeward Islands* working towards Buxton with steam to spare, in June 1951. The evening working, 5.22 pm from Manchester Central, gave many opportunities for photographs, and the train was steam worked until the end of this service in March 1967.

On 2nd July, 1932, 4-4-0 No. 489, a former Midland class '2P', passes the small fog signalman's hut having just left Pie Tor tunnel with the 4.03 pm from Manchester Victoria to Buxton. The large crane (seen over the first coach) is in position for the reconstruction of the bridge (over the River Wye) over which the train has just passed.

The original cast iron arched bridge at Pie Tor (No. 9) was replaced by a steel girder structure in July 1932, as were other bridges on the Buxton branch. The new bridge seen here was constructed on the trestle to the left, and slid into position.

When this photograph was taken in May 1933, signs of the replacement of King Sterndale Bridge had largely gone, and the 1.35 pm push-pull set from Buxton travels smoothly over the new structure.

On 29th September, 1955, the valley echoes to the beat of ex-LNWR 0-8-0 No. 49837 (from Buxton shed) as a mineral train is hauled past Topley Pike signal box, on its way to Buxton. There has been rail access to Topley Pike Quarry since 1874, though at the time of writing there is no rail traffic from the quarry, but the link to the right still exists, controlled by a ground frame.

A view from the road side (looking west) of the original Topley Pike bridge, in May 1932. Buxton 0-4-4T No. 1366 is progressing towards Buxton Junction at Blackwell Mill, with the signal 'off' for Miller's Dale. A fine lorry, registration WW 8346, travels along the A6 with a motorcycle and sidecar in pursuit!

Another view of the original Topley Pike bridge with a Johnson class '1P' 0-4-4T No. 1366 on the two-coach service between Miller's Dale and Buxton. Shortly after this picture was taken, the bridge was replaced, so here we have a timely record of the beautiful original structure.

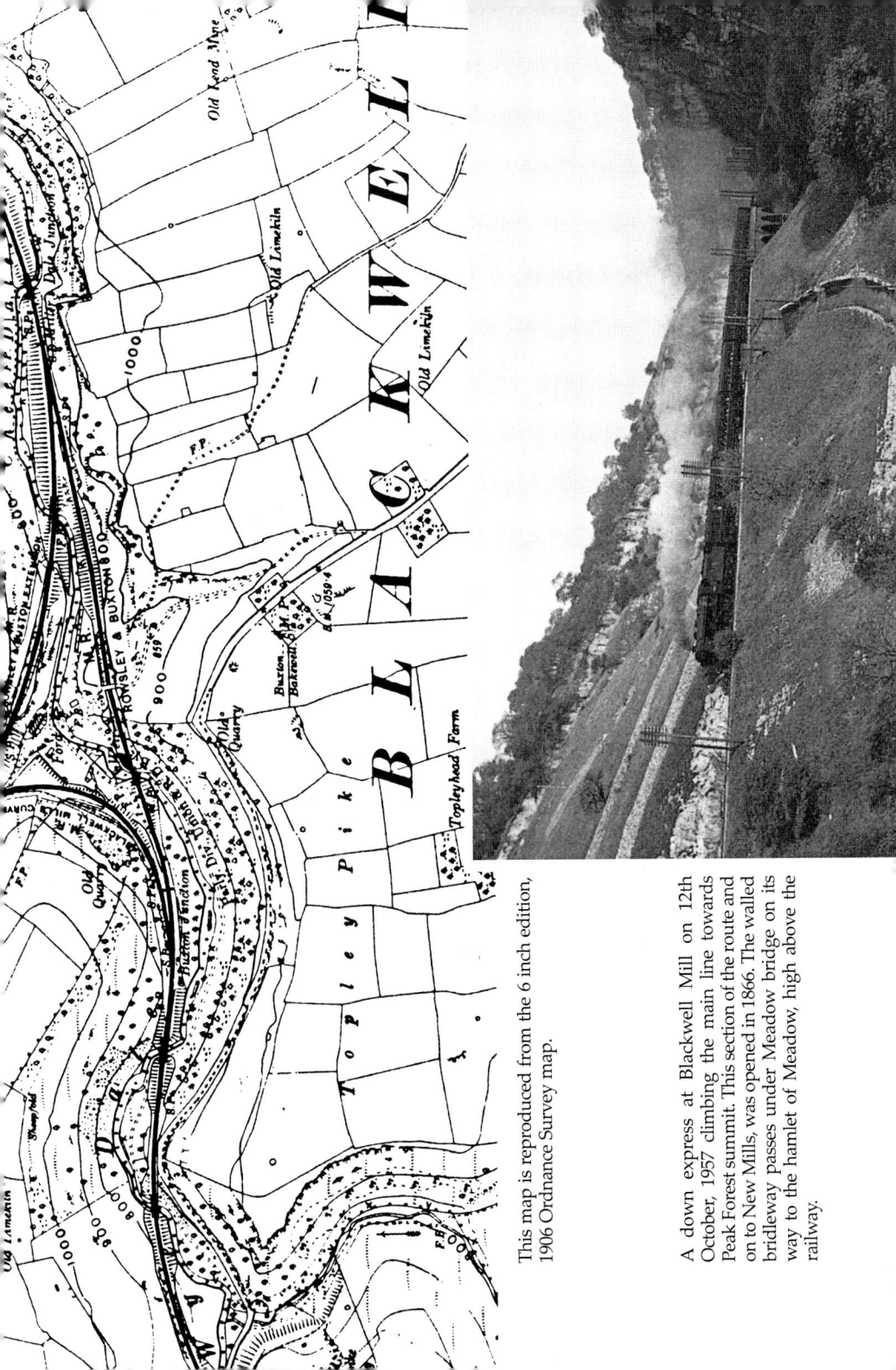

This map is reproduced from the 6 inch edition, 1906 Ordnance Survey map.

A down express at Blackwell Mill on 12th October, 1957 climbing the main line towards Peak Forest summit. This section of the route and on to New Mills, was opened in 1866. The walled bridleway passes under Meadow bridge on its way to the hamlet of Meadow, high above the railway.

A fine view on 22nd April, 1951 of the Crewe-built Stanier class '5' 4-6-0 No. 44848 passing Blackwell Mill Halt on the 10.30 am (Sundays only) Derby to Buxton service. Stanier class '8F' 2-8-0 No. 48279 waits with a full head of steam on a long freight from Gowhole.

A scene at Blackwell Mill, Buxton Junction, showing the signal box with Fowler class '4P' 2-6-4T No. 2318 accelerating past with a slow train from Buxton, on 24th June, 1948. The gradient and curve of the line to Peak Forest Junction (which the train is tackling) are quite severe.

A two car dmu passing through the diminutive Blackwell Mill Halt on 12th October, 1957. This halt served the little railway community in the Midland Railway cottages below the line, which were built in 1866 and tastefully modernised in 1970 (*see next photograph*).

Looking down from the Buxton to Bakewell road that climbs out of the dale at Topley Pike, to reach this fine panoramic viewpoint. Part of the triangular junction at Blackwell Mill can clearly be seen. A down passenger train labours past on the main line towards Manchester and approaches Peak Forest Junction tunnel. The curved line to the left links the Buxton branch to the main line at Peak Forest Junction. The River Wye winds past the cottages built by the Midland Railway Company, whilst Buxton Central Quarry dominates this 1936 scene.

At the eastern end of the triangular junction at Blackwell Mill, a double-headed down express passes Miller's Dale Junction signal box and leaves the Buxton branch to drop away, as the train continues on the main line. The pilot engine in this 30th April, 1958 view is a Stanier class '5' 4-6-0 No. 44846.

The railway was skilfully engineered through the spectacular Chee Dale, with its towering cliffs and deep cuttings. The up freight train is crossing a viaduct (No. 80) over the River Wye, as it progresses towards Rowsley in June 1948. It is easy to see why the Blackwell Mill area was a favourite location for the photographer and his sons.

Another view of Miller's Dale Junction, showing a freight train on 30th April, 1958 leaving the Buxton branch and about to join the main line. In the distance is the mouth of Rusher Cutting tunnel.

Looking from the signal box at Miller's Dale Junction we can see the splitting signals at the approach to the junction. ·The class '8F' 2-8-0 No. 8712, on a down freight, has the main line signal and will continue towards Peale Forest. The River Wye down below on the right can just be seen.

At the eastern end of Rusher Cutting tunnel (121 yards long), the 12.20 pm Manchester Central to St Pancras express, emerges on to a ledge above the River Wye, on a dull 22nd May, 1933. The locomotive is class '4P' 4-4-0 No. 1058, a three cylinder compound. This tunnel had its western portal strengthened and made as a covered way with the last 35 yard section being supported on pillars with a covered top.

Dramatic spurs of limestone are pierced by two tunnels in quick succession at Chee Tor. Here a pushpull service for Buxton is emerging from Chee Tor No. 1 tunnel, straight on to a short single arch bridge (No. 76A) high above the River Wye, before plunging into Chee Tor tunnel No. 2 (94 yards). All this happened very quickly and passengers had to be alert to catch a glimpse of a view into the dale and of the river below.

This view from high above Chee Tor No. 1 tunnel gives an impression of the rugged yet beautiful nature of the landscape and the way the line hugs the contours of the land. The express, emerging from Chee Tor No. 2 tunnel, is running 'wrong road' due to permanent way work on Sunday 1st July, 1951. In the distance, the ledge high above the River Wye and Rusher Cutting tunnel entrance can be seen.

A lineside view of the 94 yds-long Chee Tor No. 2 tunnel, photographed from just inside the mouth of the No. 1 tunnel. 'Jubilee' class 4-6-0 No. 45622 *Nyasaland*, hauls the 9.00 am (Sundays only service) from Manchester Central to St Pancras on 25th May, 1952. The River Wye below the train makes a great sweep around the bastion of rock through which the tunnels burrow.

The photographer's elder son and a friend, wearing Buxton College caps, are watching the up express leaving the 401 yards-long Chee Tor No. 1 tunnel, at its eastern end, in 1939. The locomotive is again a 'Jubilee' class 4-6-0 No. 5698 *Mars*, with a Fowler-designed narrow, straight sided 3500 gallon tender.

No. 5276, one of the very reliable and numerous Stanier-designed class '5P5F' 4-6-0 locomotives in immaculate condition, passing over the River Wye on the three-arched bridge (No. 75, the East Buxton bridge) in August 1937, on its way to Manchester. The photographer is acknowledged from the footplate! Some remnants of the East Buxton Quarry kilns, which can be seen beyond the train, are still visible from the Monsal Trail, which today follows the route of the railway.

Looking towards Miller's Dale in May 1931, with Johnson class '3F' 0-6-0 No. 3281 (a survivor from Midland Railway days) on a down freight. East Buxton signal box still stood at this time and can be seen beyond the tall outer home signal, 'off' in readiness for an up train to approach Miller's Dale station. Note the Midland Railway cast iron notices. The footpath crossing in the foreground, was a blessing for photographers.

This view shows the approach to Miller's Dale station from the west end. Trackwork for Station Quarry is seen in the foreground. The layout of the station seen in this view dates from 1905/6, following the enlargement of the earlier station and the building of a second viaduct at the eastern end. This new layout gave the station five platform edges with two up and two down lines running through. The Buxton bound push-pull service has just left platform 5, on the far right of the station complex.

A Liverpool to Nottingham train draws into Miller's Dale on 18th May, 1951. The photograph gives a signalman's view of the station as seen from the signal box. Miller's Dale was a surprisingly large station for such a rural area, however its importance was as a junction for passengers to and from Buxton, to connect with trains going directly to Manchester, London, Derby, Nottingham and Liverpool.

Small communities nearby provided some passengers, Tideswell being the nearest sizeable village, as shown on the station nameboard. The class '5XP' 4-6-0 No. 5657 *Tyrwhitt*, is preparing to stop at platform No. 1, which had the unusual feature of hosting the local post office at the end nearer to the village. Stopping trains from Miller's Dale would drop passengers off at Bakewell, Matlock, Chapel, New Mills, and many other intermediate stations. This station closed completely on 6th March, 1967.

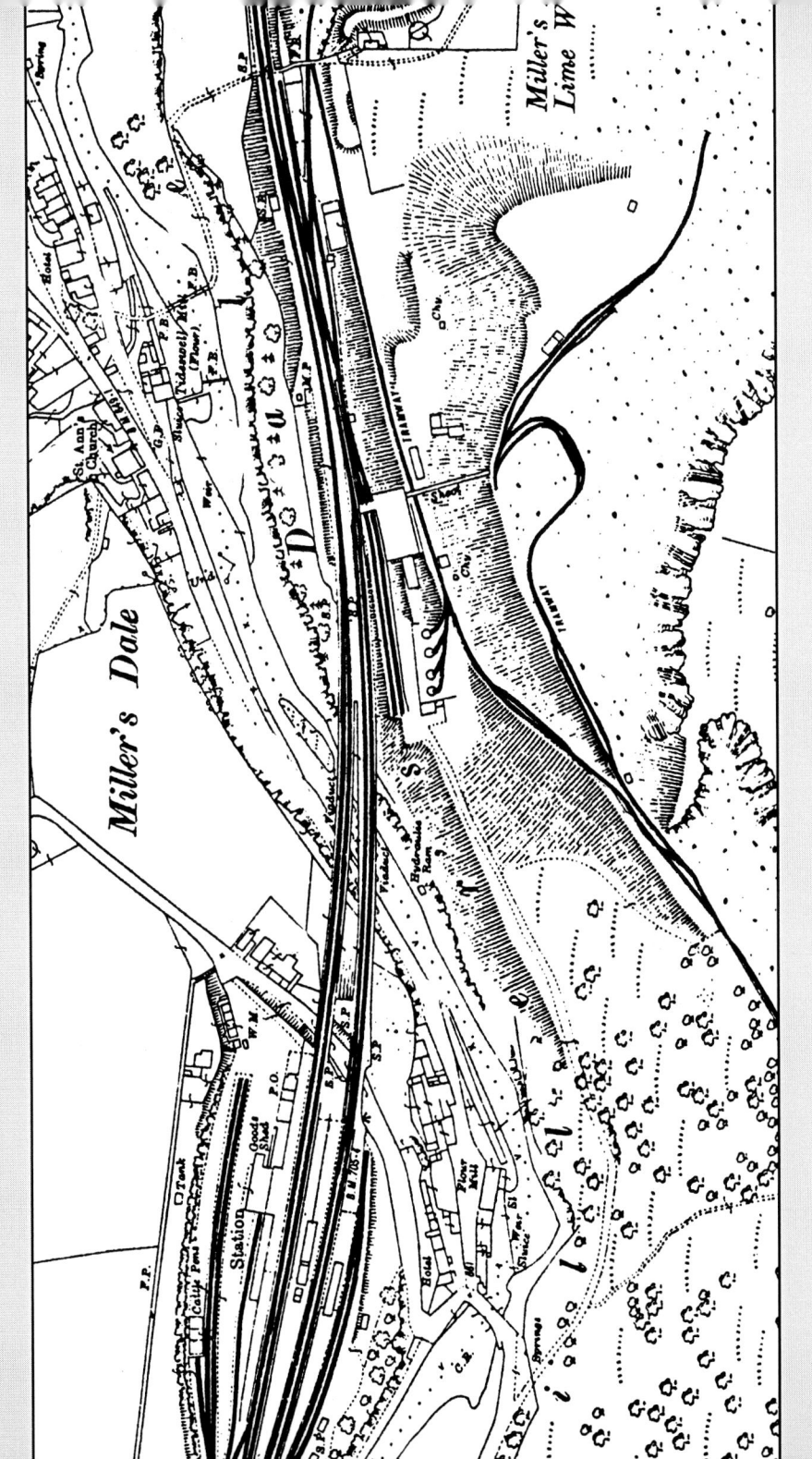

This high level view allows the reader to see the layout of Miller's Dale station, with its four through platforms and the bay. This August 1952 photograph shows 'Jubilee' class '5XP' 4-6-0 No. 45612 *Jamaica* pulling away with the 1.45 pm Manchester Central to London, St Pancras express. The local train stands in platform 5 (the bay) ready for its short journey to Buxton. The nearer of the two viaducts is the original MR structure (1863) whilst the train crosses the later 1905 viaduct. The station master's house stands prominently above the weighbridge and coal offices.

A view from platform 4, captures class '3F' 0-6-0 No. 3274 trundling through Miller's Dale on a down freight. It was often tempting for photographers and spotters to disobey the sign under the lamp here and to 'nip' over the luggage crossing to capture another train, however all the platforms were connected by a subway. The train is running over the old viaduct having just passed the workings of the Miller's Dale Lime Co. Quarry, seen in the distance. The previous view was taken from this site and today the kilns have been preserved.

The new, blue 'Midland Pullman' train, with Miller's Dale station beyond in August 1960, one month after this unique train's introduction to service. Although heralded by the railway as a success, they were known by the passengers for bad vibration and rough riding and after 1966 were transferred to the Western Region. These 'sets' made a fine sight as they flashed through the Peak District scenery. The journey time from Manchester to St Pancras was 3 hours 13 minutes.

The locomotive exchanges of 1948 saw very interesting workings all over the railway network. Here in June, ex-LNER Class 'B1' 4-6-0 No. 61251 *Oliver Bury* is seen leaving Miller's Dale with a Manchester express. Note the Buxton push-pull service in the bay platform. Another exciting visitor to the line at that time, was ex-Southern Railway 'West Country' class 4-6-2 No. 34005 *Barnstaple* (*see later*).

Class '2P' 4-4-0 No. 332 passes Miller's Dale Lime Sidings, and the signal box that controlled them, with the 12.20 pm stopping service from Chinley to Derby in September 1938. St Anne's church can be seen in the valley below, right.

A scene as high summer approaches, in June 1933. A sight long gone as a down stopping freight from Rowsley, with class '4F' 0-6-0 No. 4261 trundles around the curve near Litton, past the distant signals for Miller's Dale. Note in the far left distance, cottages connected with Litton Mill.

The distant signals seen in the previous picture, appear here again. They indicate the fast and slow roads through Miller's Dale station. The 12.25 pm service from Manchester to St Pancras picks up speed on the down gradient with class '5MT' 4-6-0 No. 5089 providing the motive power in September 1938. The exposed limestone rim of the River Wye valley can be seen on the right, showing the railway is still closely following the route of the river.

Two tunnels now occur in quick succession and this view shows Litton tunnel (515 yards). An up special hauled by a class '5MT' 2-6-0 coasts along on 27th August, 1955, high above the valley gorge, and subjected to a 50 mph track restriction at this curved section. Its passengers will have a few moments to capture the scenery before being plunged into darkness again.

This view from way above the railway looks down into the River Wye gorge known as Water-cum-Jolly Dale. The double-headed freight has just left Litton tunnel and is passing a three aspect colour light signal as it approaches Cressbrook tunnel (471 yards). The drop from the railway to the river is 90 feet at this point; the footpath seen at the left runs from Cressbrook to Litton and is a popular route for walkers. The river curves away but will be alongside the track again when the train emerges from the other end of the tunnel.

Monsal Dale station is really in Upper Dale, a part of the river valley just before Monsal Dale is reached. The up platform was a wooden construction and built on piles over the valley. The station had a loading dock siding and a 45 wagon passing loop. The station was opened on 1st September, 1866. The sparse wooden station building was moved from Evesham to keep the cost of construction down, however toilet facilities were not added until 1875. At one time the Monsal Dale Spar Mine Ltd shared the use of the goods facilities on the right. Only a few local people used the station, the latter being mainly supported by the many walkers who travelled to the area to enjoy the magnificent scenery and walks. Here Stanier class '8F' 2-8-0 No. 48215 drags a long mineral train through the station on 19th July, 1958. The station closed a year later on 10th August, 1959.

Facing page: One of the best views of the route is from above the fine, curved, five-arched Monsal Dale viaduct, which crosses the River Wye. In the distance can be seen Buckley's bridge (No. 66) and then the line ran to Cressbrook tunnel. On 29th September 1951 a down mineral train is being assisted up the steeply graded route by a banking engine attached at Rowsley. This view of Monsal and Upper Dales is much the same today, but lacks the steam, smoke and atmosphere of the working days. Visitors can now walk down to the trackbed and walk over, then under this splendid viaduct, as it is part of the Monsal Trail.

The River Wye turns through 90 degrees here and is now flowing south-west as we look against the afternoon sun at Monsal Dale, described at one time as 'The Arcadia of Derbyshire'. The class '7F' 0-8-0 has a good head of steam in readiness for the long climb ahead. An exciting feature here was the way in which the down trains would emerge without warning from Headstone tunnel (533 yards) whose portal opened directly on to the viaduct from a vertical rock face 80 foot above the river. This tunnel forms the divide between the rugged area described and the more pastoral area encountered as the route proceeds southwards from this point.

Great Longstone station is reached next; originally called Thornbridge (before the opening of the line), changed to Longstone then renamed Great Longstone in 1913. The station echoes to the sound of class '5MT' 2-6-0 No. 42874 (of Rowsley shed 17D) on a down freight on 21st April 1956. This attractive station served the adjacent villages of Longstone and Ashford-in-the-Water, plus nearby Thornbridge Hall.

Great Longstone station (once the nameboard read 'Great Longstone for Ashford'), is now an interesting feature on the Monsal Trail but at one time the peace was regularly disturbed by the many passenger and freight trains passing through! On 21st April, 1956 Stanier class '8F' 2-8-0 No. 48654 pounds through with a mixed freight. To the south of the station lies Thornbridge Hall, a neo-Tudor mansion. This was the home of George Marples, who became a director of the Midland Railway. Just behind the down platform is 'Woodlands', a house built by Marples for his staff.

This view of Great Longstone station on 15th March, 1952 shows the fine limestone-built bridges Nos. 61 and 60, with the line curving away towards Hassop. Stanier class '8F' 2-8-0 No. 48677, with its water filler lid on the tender not closed down (a common practice), coasts through on an up freight. Later in 1952 the station won the Midland Region Best Kept Station Competition, mainly for its superb flower gardens.

Hassop station was over a mile from the village of the same name that it served; however it was solidly built, in spacious, traditional MR style, largely to provide the Duke of Devonshire at Chatsworth with a station, possibly in rivalry with the Duke of Rutland, who had railway access at Bakewell. The glazed transverse-ridge canopies were removed in the 1940s and the lower photograph shows the semi-circular arches that they covered. LMS compound 4-4-0 No. 1021 slows to a halt in May 1934.

A view south from the road bridge at Hassop station captures 'Jubilee' class 4-6-0 No. 45629 *Straits Settlements* passing through with a down express, made up as usual of nine coaches. Although passenger traffic was rather sparse, it was an important centre for goods traffic with a thriving coal trade and the goods yard was substantial for the size of station. The station closed earlier than most on the line, in 1942, and now part of the up side buildings house a book shop, café and cycle hire. The station master's house, on the right, was derelict until 1986 when it became a private residence.

Here the approach to Bakewell station is seen from beside the goods yard road. Beyond the original signal box, a crowded down platform can be seen as this was Bakewell Show Day, when the railway brought in thousands of visitors. Class '5MT' 2-6-0 No. 42890, seen here on 7th August, 1958, is bringing empty stock into the station to pick up the passengers who have enjoyed a day out at the show. The coaching stock was stored far and wide on show days and freight traffic was suspended.

With a wave from the photographer's elder son, Johnson '2P' 4-4-0 No. 504 is seen piloting a LMS Compound through Bakewell station on the 12.20 pm Manchester to St Pancras express in 1934.

Bakewell station in 1963 with a permanent way train waiting to cross to the down line. Note the ornate ridge canopy over the platform, similar to that at Hassop station. Just visible over the canopy is a camping coach, once quite a familiar feature around the country. The rental for a week in Bakewell's coach was £3 10s. (£3.50) in 1934, but this had risen to £12 10s. (£12.50) by 1965. The station was over ½ mile from Bakewell's centre and being high above the town, a stiff climb was involved to reach it.

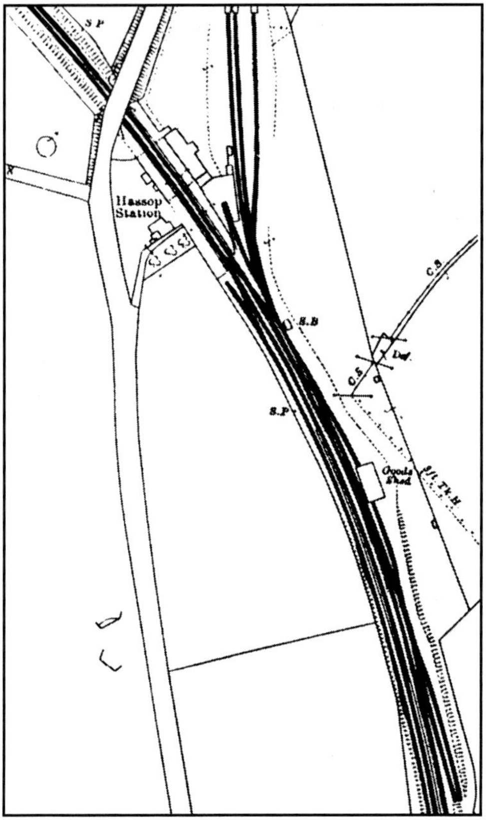

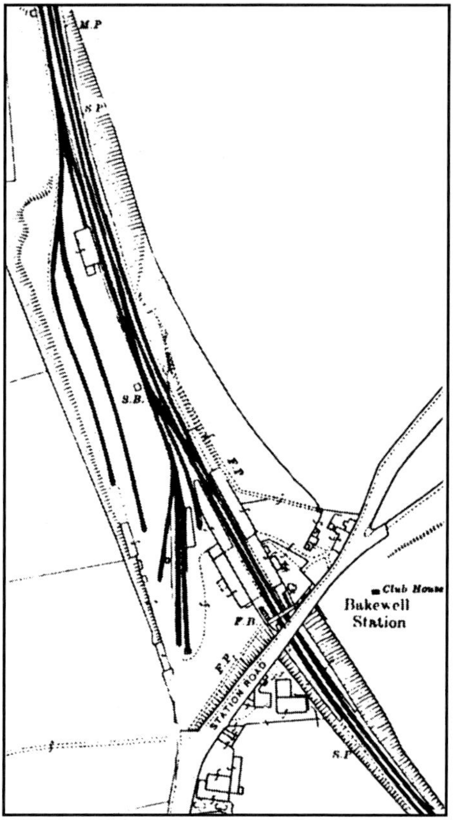

Stanier class '5MT' 4-6-0 No.45279 glides through Bakewell (a 50 mph limit existed on this section) on the 1.45 pm Manchester to St Pancras express in May 1952. Note the fine MR signal post with its two signal arms, one for each direction and capped with a typical finial.

Haddon tunnel signal box and the approach to the tunnel were set in attractive surroundings, making this a popular location for weekend photography. Here No. 44806 sweeps past on the 1.45 pm from Manchester Central. The line in the foreground was a refuge for up to 33 wagons, allowing freight trains to be passed by passenger services.

Bursting thankfully out of Haddon tunnel (1058 yards), Stanier class '8F' 2-8-0 No. 48089 climbs towards Haddon Box with a train of mineral wagons on 1st June, 1957. The refuge siding can be seen on the right. Haddon tunnel had only a small length of 'true' tunnel towards the centre, but the rest involved 'cut and cover' technique purely to hide the railway from the view of the Duke of Rutland, who insisted that the railway 'be out of sight' from his country seat of Haddon Hall nearby.

On 2nd July, 1938, Fowler class '4F' 0-6-0 No. 4019 works hard on the 1 in 102 gradient between Rowsley and Haddon tunnel. Here the line is on an embankment and Duke's Private Road Bridge (No. 45) took the lane underneath. The splitting distant signals are those for Rowsley North Junction.

The 1.45 pm from Manchester Central to St Pancras express seen entering Rowsley station in May 1935. No. 926 is a Fowler '4P' 4-4-0 3-cylinder compound. The sterling work done by these engines on the line was soon to be challenged by the Stanier 4-6-0s being built in 1935. The sharp curve through Rowsley station restricted the speed of trains to 45 mph.

Stanier class '8F' 2-8-0 No. 48198 trundles through Rowsley (for Chatsworth) on a short ballast train seen here at the southern end of the station. The 17A shed plate on the smokebox indicates this engine was based at Derby shed. Note the water column to serve the up trains.

Rowsley station (nameboard saying 'for Chatsworth') looking south. This station was the second to be built at Rowsley, being opened on 1st August, 1862 when the line was extended to Hassop. However the down platform structure (*right*) was not added until 1894. Note the glazed ridge canopies and the wooden partitions to give waiting passengers some protection from the biting winds. The original branch terminus station and engine shed were situated to the left of the photograph. The freight train has already obtained its banking engine for the long haul ahead.

Midland timetable for June 1860, showing Rowsley station as a terminus for the branch, with a note re-connecting omnibus services.

This map is reproduced from the 6 inch edition, 1906 Ordnance Survey map.

Johnson-designed class '2P' 4-4-0 No. 532 pulls past Rowsley North Junction signal box, having negotiated the tight curve through the station. The train is the St Pancras portion of the 2 pm ex-Manchester Central and the date is 12th August, 1939. The lines to the right lead to the original Rowsley branch terminus and engine shed. On the left is the north end of the large goods yard which was such a dominant feature at Rowsley.

This view shows the original Rowsley terminus station built in 1849. This remained the terminus of the line for eleven years, due to the dispute with the Duke of Devonshire over the route beyond here to the north, and lack of finance. In 1860 the MR successfully applied to Parliament to construct its own line from Rowsley to Buxton, following the River Wye.

Rowsley Sidings were opened in 1877 and until their closure in 1964 handled enormous volumes of goods traffic. Here a class '4F' 0-6-0 No. 44580, pulls its train out of the up yard past Rowsley South Junction. Rowsley has a long history as a community, but the coming of the railway and its later developments made a great impact, and many employees lived here and at Darley Dale.

In 1926, three years after the grouping of the railways and the formation of the LMS, a new engine shed was brought into use, situated just south of the goods yard. This was primarily a freight depot and the class '3' and '4Fs' seen here in 1957 were typical of the allocation to this shed. These classes were often used as banking locomotives on the steep climb to the Peak Forest.

This page shows two views of the LNWR Royal Train at Rowsley in July 1933, bringing King George V and Queen Mary on a visit to nearby Chatsworth House, seat of the Duke of Devonshire. Hauled by 'Patriot' class '5XP' 4-6-0 No. 5996, the train ran 'wrong road' into the station to avoid the Royal party having to walk through the subway at the station. The upper view shows the train arriving, whilst the lower shows the departure. The locomotive was serviced and cleaned at Rowsley shed. The Express Dairy milk tank wagons are a reminder of an important service that the railway used to undertake, now handed over to road transport.

One of the last Midland Railway-built class '4Fs' 0-6-0 No. 44013 passing Church Lane crossing, just a mile south of Rowsley South Junction with an up mixed freight on 14th September, 1957. The locomotive is working hard as it approaches the short climb through Darley Dale and is about to pass under the footbridge dated 1911.

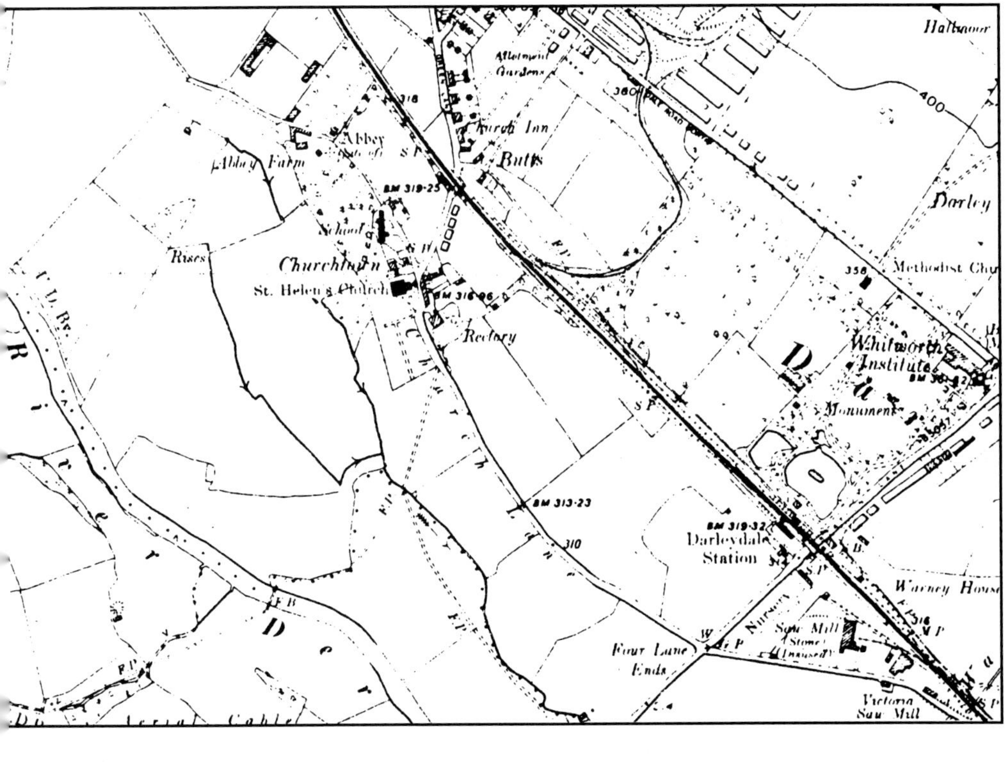

Class '4F' 0-6-0 No. 44021 with a down mineral train on 14th September, 1957, approaching Darley Dale from the south, seen here crossing the Winster road, as viewed from the footbridge. Note the camping coach behind the signal box. The sidings either side of the running lines were capable of holding well over 100 wagons. The station opened as 'Darley' on 4th June, 1849 but changed its name to Darley Dale in 1890.

Two trains at Darley Dale. *Above*; Stanier class '5P' 4-6-0 No. 5288 hurries towards the capital on an express in 1937 whilst, *below*, class '4P' 4-4-0 3-cylinder compound No. 935 pulls out from the down platform on a Manchester-bound working. Darley Dale station was reopened in 1991 by the Peak Rail PLC and it was not long before the first train ran over the re-laid section to a new station constructed at Matlock. In 1997 they extended their line from Darley Dale to Rowsey sidings about half a mile south of the village. More recently, in 2011, the line was extended south to Network Rail's Matlock station to form an interchange with the national rail service. The ambition to extend the line to Buxton remains an important part of their future plans.

Darley Dale was a popular place to visit at one time and records show that numbers of passengers were considerable in the late 1890s. Here Beyer Garratt 2-6-6-2 No. 47997 crosses the Darley Bridge road on a down freight. These locomotives were not popular with their crews but they made an impressive sight.

The unusual elevated signal box at Matlock replaced two smaller boxes in 1910. It spanned the line to the goods shed and the signalmen's climb to work involved two steep flights. Class '4F' 0-6-0 No. 44515 runs past the box with an up freight on 15th March, 1952. Some of the extensive quarry sidings at Matlock can be seen on the right Above them on the hilltop, part of Riber Castle can be seen.

Matlock is a busy town with the County Offices situated in the former 'Hydro', where water cures were offered. The railway from here to Derby still operates, but after the closure of the Peak line, Matlock lost its through services to Manchester and London. Here Stanier class '5' 4-6-0 No. 45285 approaches the station with the 1.45 pm from Manchester Central to London, again on 15th March, 1952.

Taken from the north end of the down platform at Matlock station, this photograph illustrates the period when both diesel and steam operated on the line in the 1960s. The Sulzer powered diesel, No. D9 *Snowdon* waits to move off on its trip to Manchester and a '7P' 'Royal Scot' approaches with an up express.

Just south of Matlock the line enters another scenic area and runs through a narrowing gorge, enclosed by limestone cliffs which have been formed by the course of the River Derwent. Here between a series of tunnels called High Tor Numbers 2, 1A, and 1 and Holt Lane tunnel, class '4P' 4-4-0 No. 1028 approaches Matlock with a Derby to Manchester 'slow' in August 1934. Note the private owner wagons owned by ICI (Lime) Ltd, Buxton.

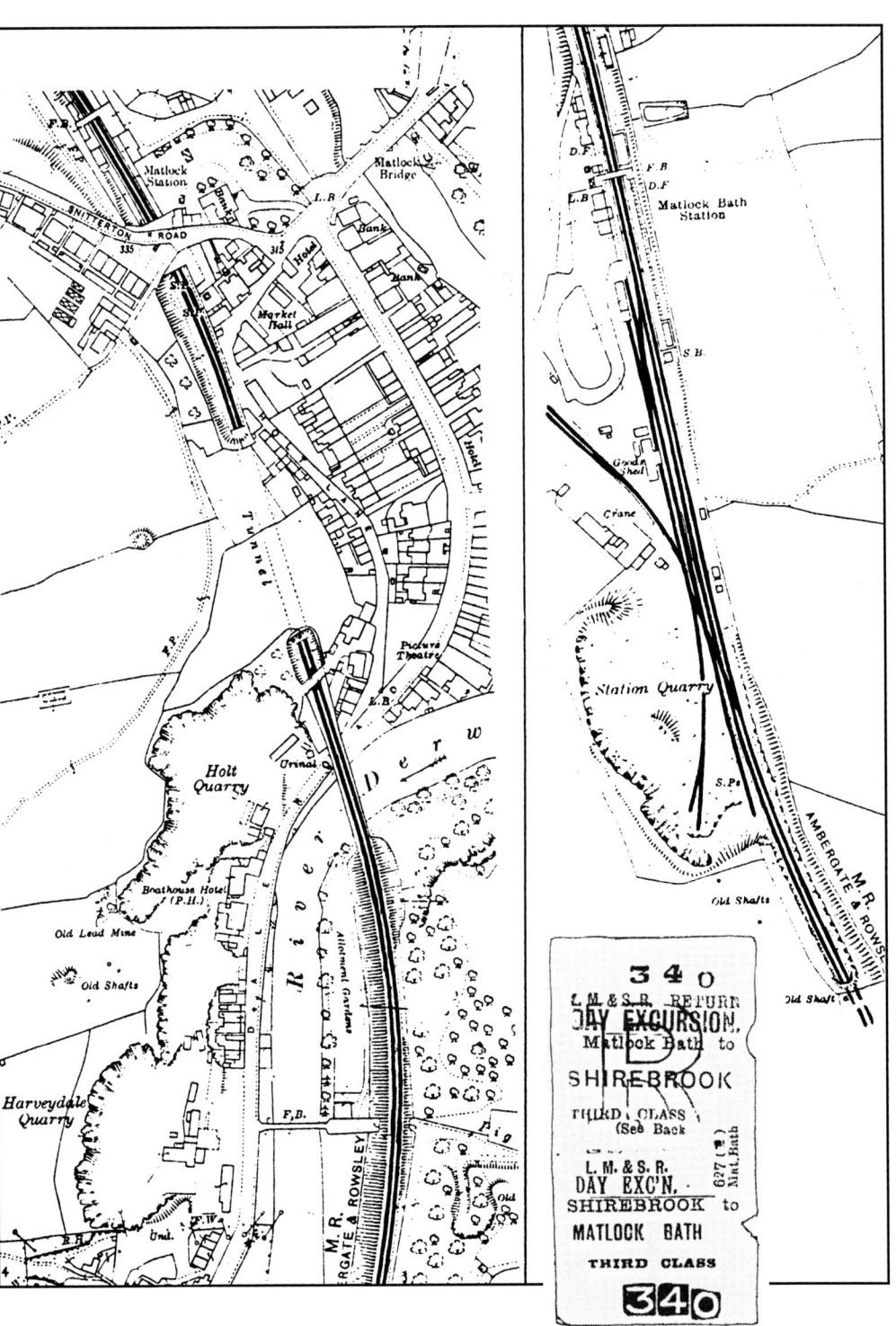

On a sunny day in May 1952, 'Jubilee' class '5XP' 4-6-0 No. 45649 *Hawkins* bursts out of High Tor tunnel and thunders through Matlock Bath station with an up express. The Derwent valley here has been named 'The Switzerland of England' and the style of the station buildings are reminiscent of Swiss chalet design. Part of the station buildings now houses the 'Whistlestop' display and shop, run by the Derbyshire Wildlife Trust.

On the same day another 'Jubilee' 4-6-0 No. 45628 *Somaliland* passes Matlock Bath signal box with a Manchester-bound express. Only a small goods yard was possible here and the compressed pointwork (*bottom right*) in the form of a double slip, allowed maximum use of the space available.

Hurrying out of the southern end of Willersey tunnel (764 yards), 'Jubilee' class 4-6-0 No. 45629 *Straits Settlements* passes through Cromford Station. Today the up line has been removed leaving only a single line to carry the traffic. Cromford station is now a listed building and still looks much the same as it did in this 1953 photograph. The National Tramway Museum is situated very near to here at Crich.

Going south from Cromford station, the railway immediately crosses the Crich Road and then the River Derwent, which the line then follows right through to Derby. This station had no sidings or signal box although there were sidings about a mile and half to the south. Seen from the footbridge, a Johnson '3F' 0-6-0 No. 3379 hauls a down freight through the station on a warm summer's day in 1934.

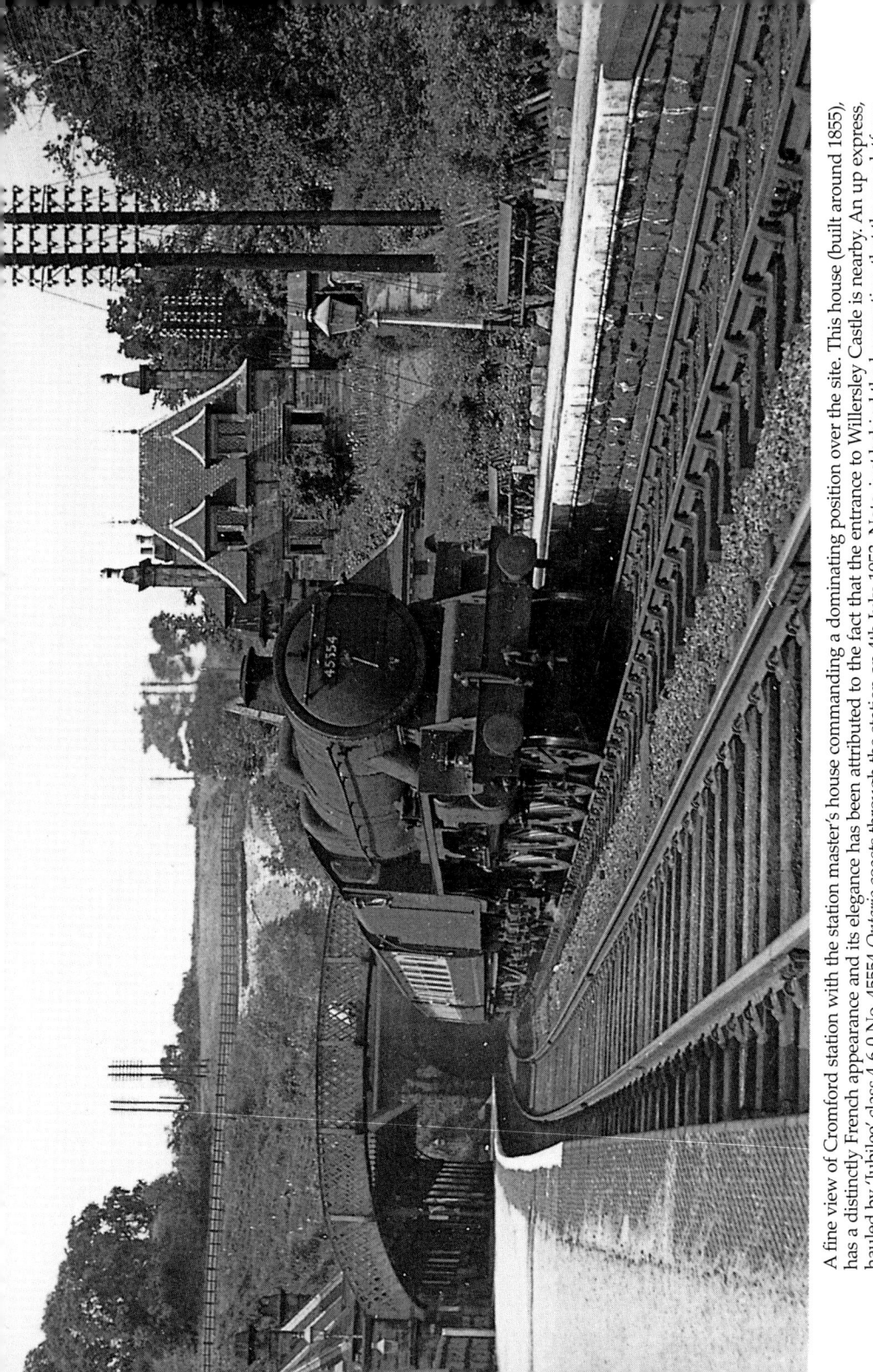

A fine view of Cromford station with the station master's house commanding a dominating position over the site. This house (built around 1855), has a distinctly French appearance and its elegance has been attributed to the fact that the entrance to Willersley Castle is nearby. An up express, hauled by 'Jubilee' class 4-6-0 No. 45554 *Ontario* coasts through the station on 4th July, 1953. Note, just behind the locomotive, that the up platform waiting shelter was also constructed in the style of the station master's house.

A last look at Cromford station with Stanier class '8F' 2-8-0 No. 48379 running hard with a down coal train in July 1953. The sidings (just out of view in the distance), mentioned previously, were used to hold freight traffic to allow the express passenger services to pass.

The Manchester-bound 'Midland Pullman' ('First class deluxe travel') left St Pancras at 6.10 pm and here, near Leawood tunnel, the train is speeding towards Cromford down distant signal (shadow in the picture). Journey time between London and Manchester was just three hours, eleven minutes, the reverse journey being three hours and thirteen minutes.

The locomotives on this double-headed up express are just crossing the 106 ft span, iron girder bridge (No. 19) which carries the track yet again over the River Derwent. The line then passes under a bridge that carries an arm of the Cromford Canal, before plunging into the curved Leawood tunnel (315 yards). The train engine is a standard compound 4-4-0 No. 1095, whilst the pilot engine is a class '2P' 4-4-0 No. 378.

Class '4F' 0-6-0 No. 44410 passing the once busy High Peak Junction on a northbound freight in 1950. The main line continues northwards towards Leawood Tunnel, again crossing the River Derwent and then passing under the Cromford Canal. The tracks on the right made the connection with the fascinating Cromford and High Peak Railway (see *The Cromford and High Peak Railway* by A. Rimmer, Oakwood Press). The Junction signal box can just be seen and beyond this the chimney to the waterworks. Today, at the bottom of the incline of the C&HPR, is the High Peak Junction Visitor Centre, well worth a visit.

Looking from the footplate of a class 'J94', working at the interchange sidings at High Peak Junction, we can see the arched girder bridge carrying the tracks over the River Derwent, the aqueduct carrying the Cromford Canal over the railway, and finally the entrance to Leawood tunnel. The C&HPR was joined to the MR here in 1853.

A stranger to the area, class 'B1' 4-6-0 No. 61360 is seen here leaving the C&HPR interchange sidings with a Railway Correspondence and Travel Society railtour. Note the High Peak Junction signal box in this photograph, taken from Homesford bridge (No. 14). Passengers rejoined the train after travelling over the C&HPR in open mineral wagons and vans!

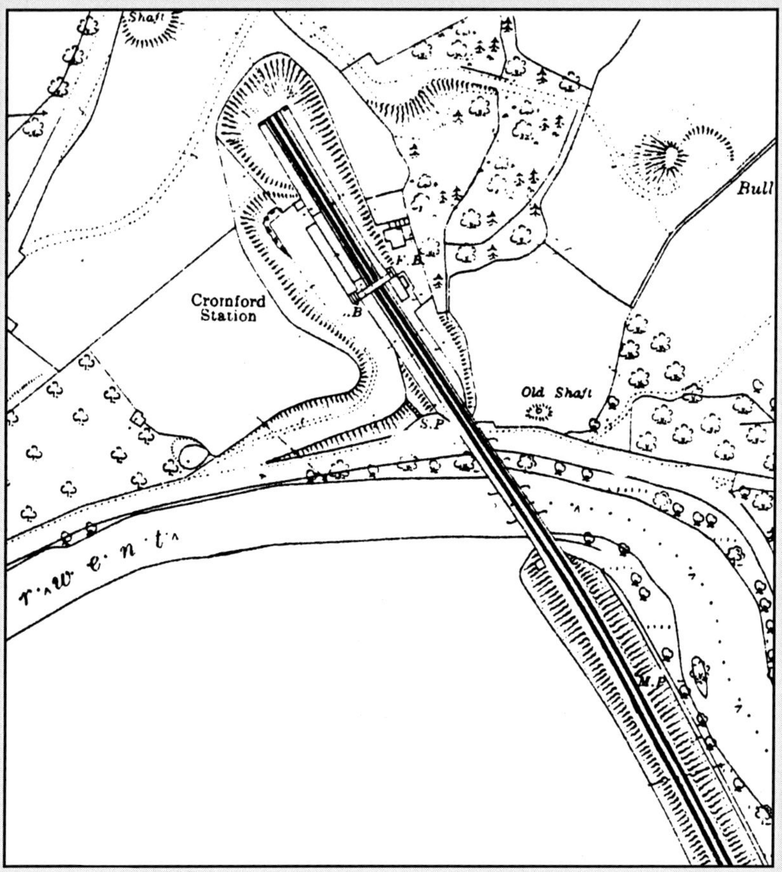
Shaft
Bull
F.B
Cromford
Station
B
Old Shaft
S.P
r w e n t
M.P

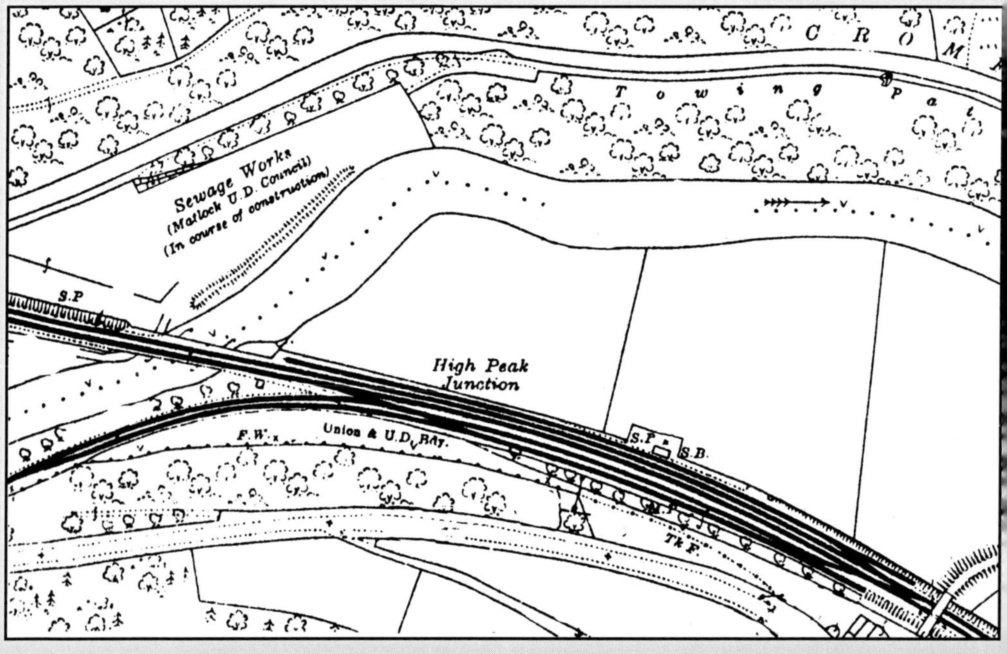
C R O M
Towing Path
Sewage Works
(Matlock U.D. Council)
(In course of construction)
S.P
High Peak
Junction
F.W.
Union & U.D. Bdy.
S.P
S.B.
M.P
Tk F.

Photographed on a sunny 24th May, 1952, from above the mouth of the 149 yds-long Whatstandwell tunnel, Stanier class '8F' 2-8-0 No. 48765 coasts past the site of the original Whatstandwell station. The Cromford Canal can be seen above the retaining wall on the right. This wall was built to support the canal when the railway was constructed here. When the second station was built, on the south side of the tunnel, this site was renamed Whatstandwell Goods. At this point the valley contains the River Derwent, the A6 road, the Peak Line and the Cromford Canal, all running in close proximity!

Viewed from the old station platform, a Stanier class '8F' 2-8-0 No. 48331 drifts past Whatstandwell signal box. Note the signal with a typical MR finial on the down line. In the distance can be seen the loading gauge for the goods yard, which over the years had seen a great deal of gritstone for building purposes pass through it. Florence Nightingale used the old station as she travelled to and from her home in Holloway, the village visible on the distant hillside.

The second station at Whatstandwell, opened in 1894. The station footbridge was linked to a footbridge over the canal, providing better access from the nearby village. The Hughes/Fowler 2-6-0 No. 13145 on this up freight, was quite a revolutionary design at this time.

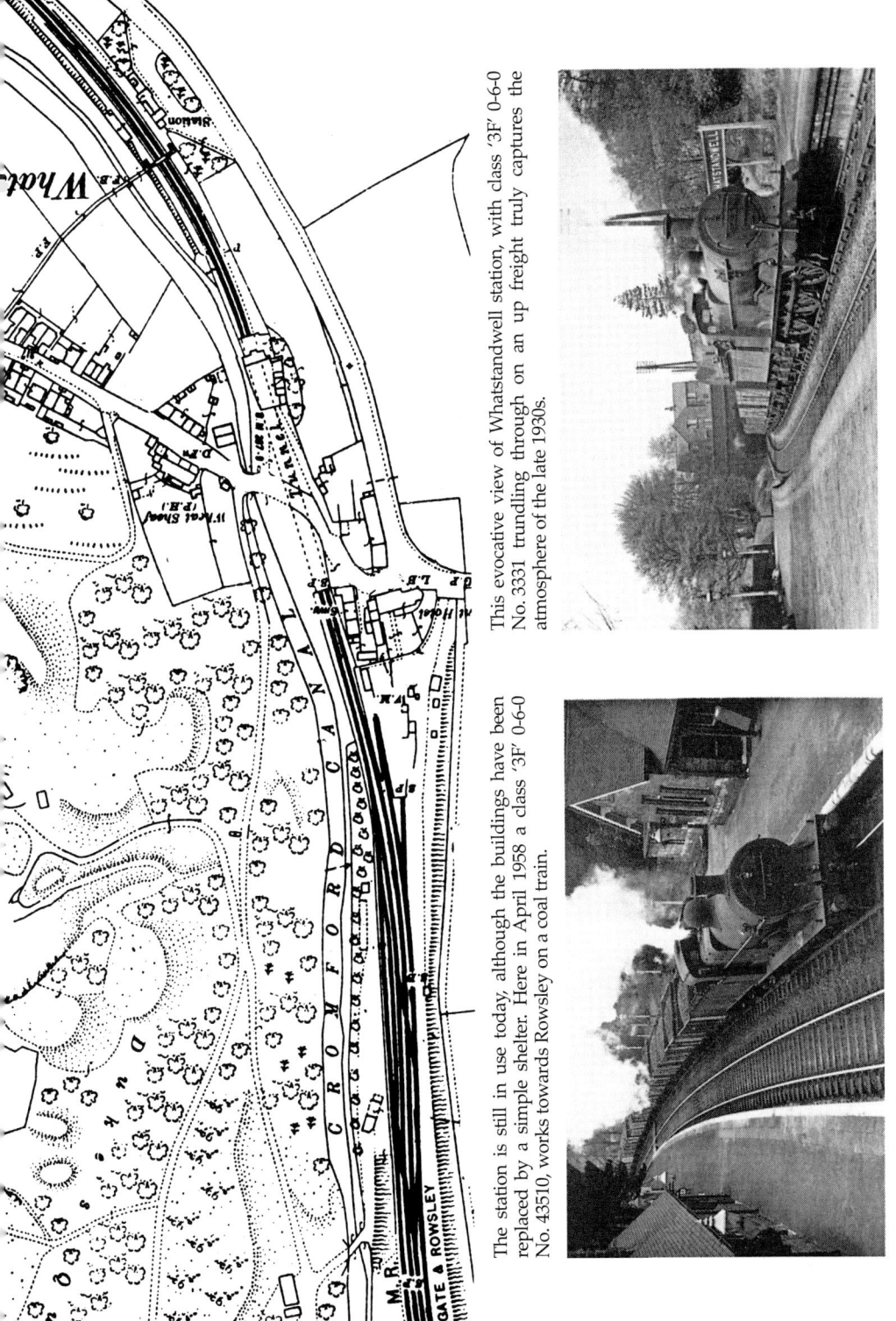

This evocative view of Whatstandwell station, with class '3F' 0-6-0 No. 3331 trundling through on an up freight truly captures the atmosphere of the late 1930s.

The station is still in use today, although the buildings have been replaced by a simple shelter. Here in April 1958 a class '3F' 0-6-0 No. 43510, works towards Rowsley on a coal train.

Storming around the approach curve towards Whatstandwell station, Stanier class '8F' 2-8-0 No. 48379 hauls a well loaded coal train on 24th May, 1952. The trackside platelayers' hut reminds us of the vital work of the track gangs, who took great pride in this stretch of line.

Johnson's Wireworks Sidings seen here on 30th April, 1933 with a class '4F' 0-6-0 No. 4042 hauling an empty 98 wagon train. The yard on the left served the wireworks nearby and was capable of handling 32 wagons. Access was controlled by Johnson's Sidings signal box between 1920 and 1933; a ground frame replaced the box in the latter year.

We reach the southernmost part of our journey (with a flourish) as the line curves majestically into Ambergate station. The station in its final form (1876) was one of only four in Britain that had platforms on all three sides of a triangle (*see map*). Lines arrive here from Derby (S), Matlock (NW) and Chesterfield (E). Here we see a very long, mixed down freight negotiating the sweeping curve on to the Peak Line. There is still a MR signal at the West Junction in this 1960 photograph.

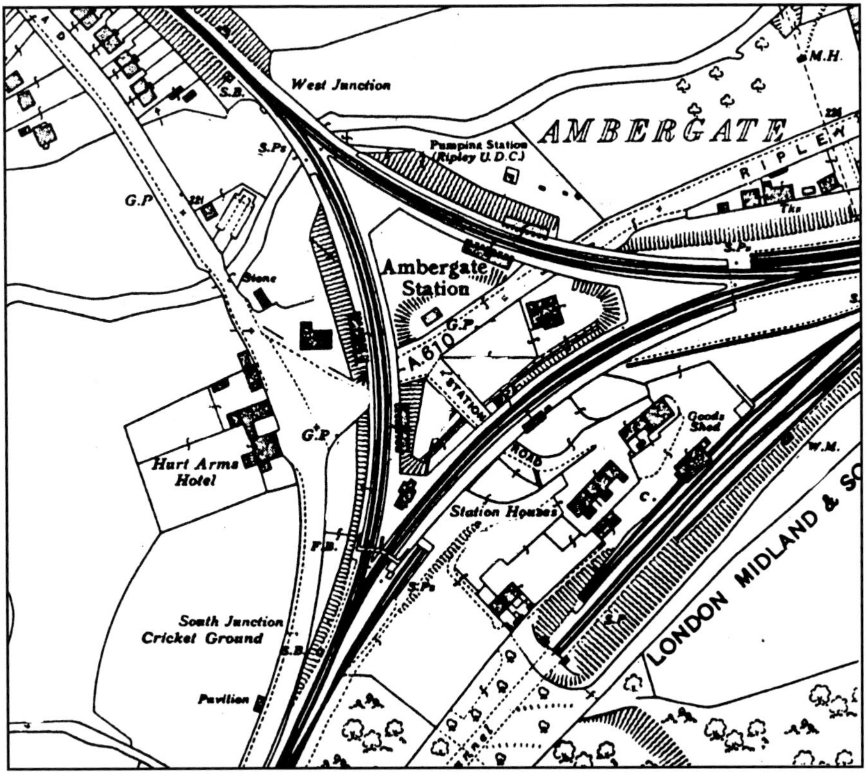

The River Amber joins the River Derwent here and Ambergate has been referred to as 'The Gateway to the Peak District'. Arriving at platform No. 2 (*right*), an up express from Manchester *en route* to Derby in 1937; class '4F' 0-6-0 No. 4407 at its head. Note how the station buildings and the rear of the platforms are all supported on piles. The station nameboard on the left reads: 'This way for Matlock, Rowsley, Buxton, Guidebridge, Liverpool and Manchester'. At this station the line joins the earlier North Midland line between Derby and Leeds, built by George Stephenson.

A Blackpool to Leicester special pulls though Ambergate on 20th August, 1960 with class '4F' 0-6-0 No. 44262 from Coalville depot in charge. Note the variety of the coaching stock. It was in 1849 that the 'Little Railway with a Big Name' - The Manchester, Buxton, Matlock and Midland Junction Railway opened between Ambergate and Rowsley. The Midland Railway Centre is located near to Ripley, not far from Ambergate and is well worth a visit.

Another similar view at Ambergate taken in 1937 showing a double-headed freight passing through platform 2 with class '4F' 0-6-0 No. 4429 piloting another unidentified class '4F'. Just above the nameboard (on the skyline) was the site of the limestone quarries at Crich and a tramway ran down the hillside, just to the right of this view to bring limestone to the limeworks at Bullbridge.

Blackwell Mill, where we start the northern leg of our journey. The main line to Manchester branched off the Buxton line at Miller's Dale Junction continued past the Buxton Central Lime Works and on to Peak Forest Junction: The view we see here on 17th April, 1960 was taken from above Peak Forest tunnel (29 yards). The line disappearing off to the right is the arm of the triangle used by Buxton-bound trains from the north. In the distance, part of the third arm of the triangle can be seen, this being the Buxton to Miller's Dale route.

Still at Peak Forest Junction, but looking north-west, we see class '4F' 0-6-0 No. 4286 with an up Sunday special in 1930 leaving the short Peak Forest tunnel and passing the Junction signal box, as it heads down to Miller's Dale Junction.

The consistent purity of the limestone in this area, with its very high calcium carbonate content, resulted in extensive quarrying. Part of the massive Tunstead Quarry, where the limestone beds are 125m thick, can be seen here. Since 1936, trains of purpose-built bogie hopper wagons have been a feature of the quarry and are seen here, as they make their way to Winnington in Cheshire. This view captures a class '8F' 2-8-0, heading a train of 16 full hoppers out of the quarry on 14th September, 1956.

The same train with a class '4F' 0-6-0 as banker, now out on the main line, heading north and just about to enter Great Rocks tunnel. Part of the elevated quarry floor and some parts of the plant at Tunstead can be seen.

On 24th June, 1959, class '2' Co-Bo Metro-Vickers diesel No. D5714 bursts out of the northern end of the 161 yards-long Great Rocks tunnel, *en route* for Chinley.

Great Rocks Junction was a favourite location for the photographer, being easily accessible from Buxton. This view from the signal box shows compound class '4P' 4-4-0 No. 1009 climbing past the ICI 'South Shops', with a down Manchester express in September 1938. The lower arm of the pair of signals controlled the entry to a long running loop just beyond the road bridge that crosses here.

Another view of Great Rocks Junction, looking north this time from the road bridge, to capture the first day in service of the 'Midland Pullman' on 4th July, 1960. The track going off to the right led to a turntable, together with a water crane and ash disposal facilities.

Just under a mile further north, the line reaches Peak Forest station, seen here in June 1966. The station was much nearer to the community of Peak Dale than to the village of Peak Forest. The station closed to passenger traffic in March 1967. As this photograph and map overleaf shows, Peak Forest was a mass of sidings and quarry lines, some of which remain today.

Peak Forest station looking northwards with the road bridge dominating the view; a footbridge was never provided at this station. On 21st September, 1959, an Officers' Special passes through, pulled by very recently restored compound class '4P' 4-4-0 No. 1000, resplendent in Midland Railway livery. The large building on the right is the Smalldale Crushing plant of the Buxton Lime Firms Company Ltd, whilst the grinding plant can be seen through the bridge arch.

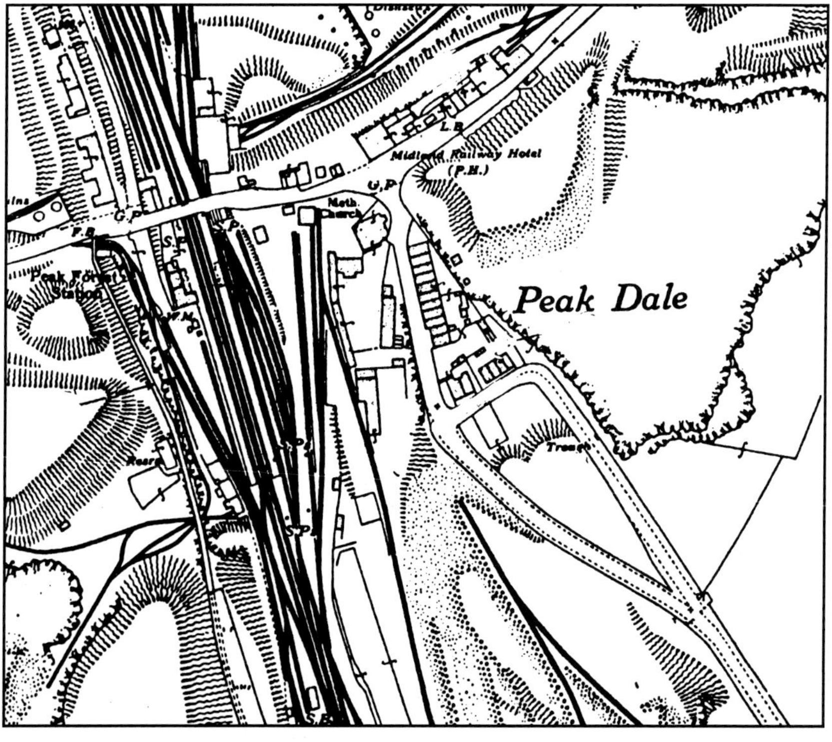

The heavily industrialised nature of the area can be seen in this view from the road bridge at Peak Forest station. Stone crushing and grinding plants are situated next to the line, and active quarrying still provides considerable traffic for the line. On 8th September, 1956, a Stanier class '8F' 2-8-0 No. 48711 returns to Tunstead Quarry with a load of empty hoppers.

The class '8Fs' were the chief 'work horses' for the stone traffic from Tunstead quarry from 1938 until the diesels took over. Here, in April 1953, No. 48406 works hard hauling a full train of hoppers as it approaches Peak Forest Summit (985 ft above sea level). The signal box closed in August 1968 shortly after the end of passenger services.

Just clear of the south end of Dove Holes tunnel (2984 yards), the crew of class '4P' 4-4-0 No. 41143 will welcome the fresh air after climbing at 1 in 90 through the long tunnel. The train is the 11.35 am from Manchester Central to Nottingham on 23rd May, 1952. The tunnel has caused engineering problems right from its construction, when (in 1864) work had to stop due to excessive water entering the workings.

The up 'Midland Pullman' (8.50 am from Manchester Central), has just left Dove Holes tunnel and is passing through the impressive cutting towards the Peak Forest Summit The picture was taken just after the introduction of the service to the route.

At the northern end of Dove Holes tunnel, Fowler class '4P' 2-6-4T No. 2382 emerges into the evening sunshine with the 7.18 pm Buxton to Chinley local service, in 1939. An extra 70 yards of covered way was built here in 1866 following a landslide; the flat area over the tunnel can be clearly seen. Note the signal with an up home, shunting arm and down distant all on the same post.

The landscape has changed dramatically during the journey through the tunnel and now gritstone moors and outcrops dominate the scene. Looking down from the southern portal of LNWR tunnel, we see another Fowler 2-6-4T on a Buxton to New Mills local train. The photographer is above the short (104 yards-long) tunnel that carries the Midland route beneath the LNWR Buxton to Manchester line. The unusual position of the up signal (by the end of the train on the right), partway up the side of the cutting, is to improve the sighting for the crews of up trains. The signal box is Dove Holes Tunnel North.

The next station to be reached is Chapel-en-le-Frith Central and here Standard class '5' 4-6-0 No. 73002 pulls away with the 2.05 pm (Sundays) from Manchester to Derby stopping service on 15th March, 1953. Chapel is a market town with a long and interesting history, at one time having a busy livestock market. The railway transported large numbers of cattle, loading and unloading taking place at a cattle dock situated at the Manchester end of the station.

The signal box on the up platform was built in 1905, to replace two other boxes, north and south of the station. The station building was very similar to those at Rowsley, Bakewell and Hassop. Class '4F' 0-6-0 No. 44144, from Heaton Mersey shed, runs through Chapel Central with what was known as the 'cabbage' train in August 1958.

Soon after leaving Chapel-en-le-Frith, the line reached the signal gantry which controlled the alternative routes at Chinley South Junction. This down express with 'Jubilee' class 4-6-0 No. 45614 *Leeward Islands* in charge, has the Manchester line signals 'off', on 4th August, 1951.

On the same day and photographed from the same bridge (but now looking northwards) we see Chinley South Junction with the Sheffield line sweeping away to the east over one of the massive viaducts at Chapel Milton. The 1.45 pm from Manchester has just crossed another impressive 15-arched viaduct, which stands across Black Brook and the A624 road, and is passing the Junction signal box with 168 miles to go to the capital.

On Sunday 15th June, 1958, the 2 pm Manchester to London express is diverted on to the Hope Valley and Sheffield line at Chinley North Junction. Class '6P' 4-6-0 No. 46152 ('Royal Scot') *The Kings Dragoon Guardsman* carefully negotiates the junction.

Chinley North Junction signal box is seen here from an up train on 29th June, 1968, the last Saturday of through running on the route to Matlock. From 1st July, 1968, passenger services were diverted to the Hope Valley line. The box which controlled this important junction was replaced by a more modem structure in 1982.

The four track approach to Chinley North Junction was an impressive location for photographers. With the hills around Chinley forming a picturesque back-drop, the 1.35 pm relief from Manchester Central is hauled by 'Jubilee' class 4-6-0 No. 45636 *Uganda* on 30th July, 1955.

And so to Chinley. A scene during the 1948 locomotive exchange trials, shows an exciting visitor to the line – Southern Region 'West Country' class 4-6-2 No. 34005 *Barnstaple* approaching Chinley station. The goods shed on the extreme right was a relic of the first station at Chinley, which was superseded in 1902 by a much larger station.

The 1902 station had five through platforms and a bay platform at the eastern end which was used by the Buxton, Derby and Sheffield local services. With its refreshment room and waiting rooms, Chinley was an impressive station and a true junction for passenger services. In the mid-1930s, 38 down and 40 up trains called daily. In March 1953, the 9.00 am from Manchester Central (Sundays only) pulls away behind 'Jubilee' class 4-6-0 No. 45629 *Straits Settlements*.

An evocative photograph of an immaculate class '4P' 3-cylinder compound 4-4-0 No. 927, leaving Chinley station for Manchester on 18th June, 1932. In the distance every platform has a train standing, showing just what a busy and important junction this station was. As the train continues on its way towards Manchester, our journey over the wonderful Peak Line comes to an end!

The Line in 1993

On 6th August, 1993, class '150' 'Sprinter' 150229 approaches Matlock station with the 14.06 arrival from Derby.

The same unit awaits departure on the 14.23 service to Derby. At Matlock, passengers can transfer to the preserved Peak Rail PLC line, on the days when services are operating.

A further view of 150229 at Matlock Bath station on the 11.48 Matlock to Derby service running under the banner of Regional Railways.

The Line in 2019

Class '153' Sprinter No. 153357 beside the newly installed glass screen at Matlock station. The screen was erected by a partnership of East Midlands Railway, Cross Country, the Derwent Valley Community Rail Partnership and Community Rail Network.

No. 153357 leaves the station on its way towards Derby, leaving behind the train hauled by Peak Rail's No. 72. Station adopters supported by the Derwent Valley Community Rail Partnership planted and maintain the flowers that grace the station. The partnership promotes the Derwent Valley Line and supports all the station volunteers. They include local residents, parish and town councils, community groups and schools who take pride in creating welcoming and attractive station environments.

No. 72 waiting by Peak Rail's platform at Matlock. The locomotive was built in 1945 and spent its working life at collieries in County Durham. It was sold in 1972, to the Colne Valley Railway, for preservation. It was restored in 2013 and is now owned privately and hired to heritage railways.

Photographs courtesy Paul Webster